Beverley Shand.

Ready, Steady, **SHIFT**

Please circle the Y = yes or the N = no, in answer to the following questions.

Ready

There is time in my life to invest in my own development	Y or N
A gap exists between where I want to be and where I am right now	Y or N
I can work on tasks that will help me to develop and grow	Y or N

Willing

I am willing to perform whatever is necessary to reach my goal and aims	Y or N
I am willing to SHIFT in my thinking concerning relationships and marriage	Y or N
I am willing to attempt new ways of achieving my goals	Y or N

Able

I have the commitment I need to succeed	Y or N
I have the support I need to make significant changes to my life	Y or N
I am mentally ready for a different approach to my life	Y or N
I am physically prepared for the encounters I may not have experienced before	Y or N

7-10 Y This program will be effective, exciting and rewarding for you

5-7 Y You may need to make some adjustments before starting this program

1-5 Y You are not interested in SHIFTING!

What do you want to get from this program?---

EYE TO EYE

Use the notes sections in this workbook to make notes whilst the facilitator takes you through the session.

Please take this book away with you to refer to as necessary in the future.

! **Did you know** that there are around 250,000 marriages in Britain each year costing around £2.5Bn
No-one gets married expecting to get divorced (unless it's a business arrangement). However, at a ratio of nearly 1 in 2 and costing around £40,000 per couple, there are around 115,000 divorces every year.

OUR AIM
Relating—and the quality of our relationships—is of deep, natural, and inherent concern for all of us and like any human endeavour, takes attention, care, and commitment. This program is designed to help you create a SHIFT in your thinking that supports the building of strong relationships allowing you to flourish whether single or married.
For those that are already married, it could serve as a means of identifying where things may have gone wrong and a platform for making things better.

In this event, you'll discover a possibility of being related independent of your past, your expectations, your preferences, or your views—a dimension more powerful than personality or circumstance—a dimension where relationships can become an occasion for creativity, vitality, intimacy, and self-expression.

Marriage Beyond Expectations:

- We offer specialist programs covering various aspects of improving relationships.
- We also offer Mediation/ Conflict Resolution service & Relationship Coaching
- Get in touch on 07957125137 or hello@marriagebeyondexpectations.com

Do not be conformed to this world, but be transformed by the renewal of your mind, that by testing you may discern what is the will of God, what is good and acceptable and perfect. Romans 12:2 ESV

Our quest is to wage war on diseased thinking and to embed the divine truth.

Life is a journey with a pre-set destination.

For I know the thoughts that I think toward you, saith the Lord, thoughts of peace, and not of evil, to give you an expected end. **Jeremiah 29:11 KJV**

The writer of the Book of Proverbs says, "*wisdom is the principle thing, and in all your getting, get understanding.*" In other words at the top of our Bucket List of things to do in our lifetime – wisdom and understanding should be at the top.

Without knowing the purpose of a thing abuse is inevitable – Myles Munro

Everything on this planet revolves around people. Our ability to rule and have dominion is linked to our connectedness to each other.
Then God said, "Let Us make man in Our image, according to Our likeness; let them have dominion over the fish of the sea, over the birds of the air, and over the cattle, over all the earth and over every creeping thing that creeps on the earth." Genesis 1:26 NKJV

Without understanding the purpose of our connections, abuse (misuse) will always result.

Be it a marriage, family or work; central to our connectedness, and being a feature in every great relationship is the ability to connect and communicate effectively.

Big Question

With its twists and turns, ups and downs, joys and pains - As we journey through life together, are we really seeing eye to eye?

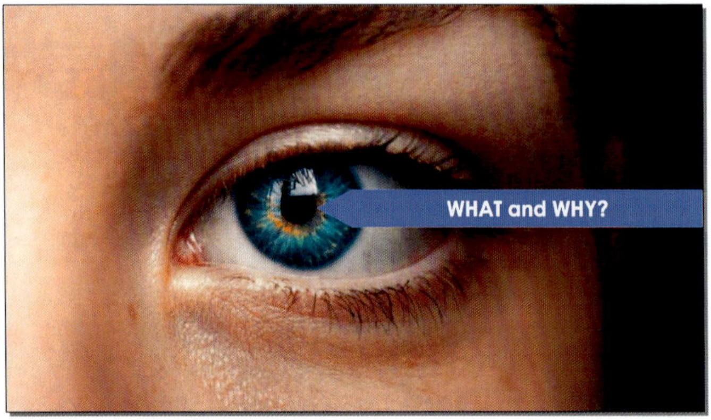

What do we mean by EYE 2 EYE?

The first relationship mentioned in the Bible doesn't include mankind but is significant in laying a foundation for us. The first three verses of Genesis gives us a picture of the most perfect relationship. Father, Spirit and Son.

- The Spirit hovering over the waters (sets the atmosphere)
- The Father speaks what He wants to see (releasing creativity)
- The Son delivers the Father's word (brings it to pass by action)

Whoa...! You may say there is no mention of the Son in Genesis 1...

You'll find this in mentioned in John 1:1-3 and Colossians 1:16-17 which clearly states that the Son was involved in creation.
He was part of the "let us (plural) make man..."

The trinity was demonstrated from the beginning - three distinct beings in one – working as one, for one purpose.

Power, creativity and fruitfulness is the result of speaking words in the right atmosphere.
This triune nature of God (tri = three, and une = united), and the fact that we were created in His image and likeness, sets the stage and benchmark for us in our human relationships.

As a man thinks so is he... Proverbs 23:7
Guard your mind with all diligence for out of it flows the issues of life Proverbs 4:23
These two passages help us to understand a simple, yet profound fact of life - you look like your thoughts. Therefore, the condition of our marriages and other relationships are directly related to how we see things individually and together.

The global purpose of God's creation is to bring increase and produce fruit. *Then God blessed them, and God said to them, Be fruitful and multiply; fill the earth and subdue it; have dominion* Genesis 1:28a

Two people are better off than one, for they can help each other succeed. Ecclesiastes 4:9 NLT

This is not just for marriage, but a concept covering all relationships

The scriptures tell us that "*two can't walk unless they agree*" and we start relationships like marriages, friendships, jobs or join churches with high hopes and expectations for the future.

However, it is our underlying thinking about situations that will determine our actions – leading to success or failure.

What is the significance of the eyes?

"*The lamp of the body is the eye. If therefore your eye is* good**, your whole body will be full of light. 23 But if your eye is bad, your whole body will be full of darkness. If therefore the light that is in you is darkness, how great is that darkness!* Matt 6:22-23 NKJV

*The word *good* means unfolded, single – referring to a single (undivided) focus, i.e. without a (secret) "double agenda" which prevents an over-complicated life (becoming needlessly distracted).

EYE 2 EYE speaks of our approach to relationships and how well we are connected. For two or more people to be in agreement, their heart condition and mindset needs to be aligned – it is this alignment without secret agendas that produces fruit...

It speaks of fellowship, and as an illustration if we consider the famous annual boat race between Oxford & Cambridge Universities. Each team has 8 men with the addition of a coxswain.

The cox as they're usually called is responsible for steering the boat and coordinating the power and rhythm of the rowers.

Maximum speed is reached when all rowers are rowing in the same direction and at the same beat/ rhythm.

Big Question

In your marriage or other significant relationships, are you rowing in the same direction?

If not, what actions will you to take to make this a reality?

List the areas that would benefit from a new rhythm and the actions you will take.

The Tower of Babel serves as an example of what's possible when people see eye to eye.
And the Lord said, "Indeed the people are one and they all have one language, and this is what they begin to do; now nothing that they propose to do will be withheld from them. Genesis 11:6

In the example above, God himself had to intervene to thwart the product of their unity.

To produce fruit takes work. Work requires energy, or you may want to call it power.
Power can be categorised as finite self-effort energy (flesh) or God's power (spirit) supplying a limitless energy to get things done.

Make no mistake, to make relationships effective/succeed takes work! Wouldn't it be better and easier when plugged into God's supply?

Unity produces power for relationship effectiveness.

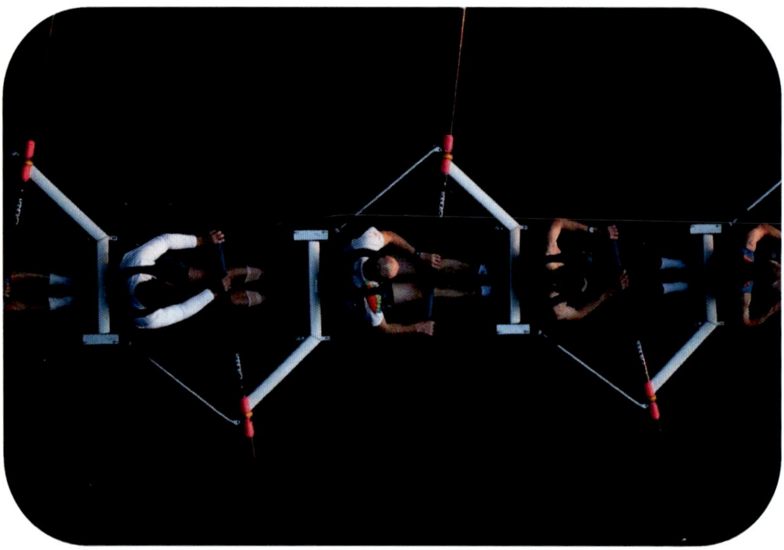

This is called the communication age, so we could easily be led to believe that we should be good at it!

Communication is a two-way process in which we both send and receive messages – it's a process of exchange.
Effective communication is when; the recipient receives all of what you were trying to send in its entirety.

1. Think of a time with your spouse or other significant relationships when you experienced them not meaning what they actually said.
2. Have you said something to someone and they got the wrong end of the stick?

There are 3 basic types of communication: words, tone of voice and body language.

- Words are only part of the message, in that people don't always say what they mean.
- Tone gives deeper meaning to the words spoken.
- Body language is an excellent indication of how people really feel.

More than words

Below are some other ways we communicate with those we are connected to:

Positive	Negative
Acts of Service	Acts of Selfishness
Physical Touch	Physical Touch
Quality Time	Lack of Time
Words of Affirmation	Silence
Giving of Gifts	Withholding

Big Question **Is your message being received as you intended it?**

Any discussion about communication is incomplete without looking at listening…

PEOPLE DON'T HEAR WHAT YOU SAY, THEY INTERPRET WHAT YOU SAY

Consider this example, I have good natural vision however if I were to borrow my friend's bifocal spectacles, my vision and what I perceive now becomes affected.
We often see life through a filter of conditioning where we'll delete, distort or generalise the information around us, creating perceptions and reactions based on our own personal reality.

Deletion – Recounting a story of an event to a friend and selectively remembering only some of the detail – particularly the information that's self-serving.
Distortion – The alteration of material facts. You've eaten dinner at someone's house you compliment them on how delicious it was, you say it was so nice you could have eaten more only for them to say that you said there wasn't enough food.
Generalisation – Drawing global conclusions based on one or two experiences. Being hurt in a previous relationship, could lead to a notion that all relationships are like that.

In the examples above another person could experience the same situation at the same time and come up with a different perspective.

NOTES

Ani Poh or Hieni? These two Hebrew words are linked to effective communication.

Ani Poh means "I'm here" – for example, you are speaking to your partner and they are texting and grunting back – your mind was elsewhere.
Hineni means "Here I am" – fully immersed in the moment.

Hineni is uttered most often in response to God but it is also spoken from one individual to another. In the Bible, each time the word Hineni is used, it signifies a turning point, a potentially life-changing moment requiring decision, action and resolution.
When used in scripture, the person speaking is saying: *"I hear your call. I understand what you are asking of me. And I am prepared and ready to do it, because I recognise, although it is hard, it is also important that I act."*

The person who can say Hineni understands that it means being fully attentive, non-judgmental and emotionally available, revealing one's whole self in the moment. We hear this word when we are loved, and we say it when we love. When it is absent, we are miserable. When it is said insincerely, we feel betrayed. **Can you imagine a time when you experienced the sincere attention and attentiveness of another person? When they put themselves aside to be entirely available to you?**
We know when we are speaking to someone whose attention is not entirely on us when for example their eyes are focused elsewhere. All of us can detect the nuances that accompany this word — echoes of falsehood or distraction as well as tones of truth and sincerity.

So Jacob called the name of the place Peniel, saying, "For I have seen God face to face, and yet my life has been delivered." Genesis 32:30

FACE TO FACE – So often our relationships are governed by covert motives and behaviours designed to protect us from harm. Just like it's easier to have physical intimacy to emotional and spiritual intimacy, many of our relationships are based on surface attention as we hold aspects of our lives and feelings back.
It was only when Jacob was alone and had to let go of all the external things, that he came face to face with the presence of God and had an experience that would change his life forever.
Your marriage and other significant relationships will be forever transformed when you let go of all the external stuff and be truly vulnerable in order to hear the heartbeat of the other person.
It is therefore important to remove distractions and distracting elements to have true eye 2 eye relationships.

Jacob had previously used the word "hineni" (Genesis 27) in a disingenuous way in order to deceive (people make promises of commitment, but at times this is based on what they want and not on a genuine heart, but with a covert agenda).

Types of listening

1. Ignoring	2. Pretend	3. Selective
4. Attentive	5. Empathetic	

What is Empathy?

- It's the ability to step into the shoes of another person, aiming to understand their feelings and perspectives, and to use that understanding to guide our actions.
- Not to be confused with *"Do unto others as you would have them do unto you."*
- Empathy is about discovering difference in another person.

Complete the personal analysis of your listening habits

When in a communication situation with your spouse or other significant relationship, do you:		Seldom	Some times	Most of the time
1	Develop your response while the other person is speaking?			
2	Suspend your judgement of the person's appearance and delivery?			
3	Interrupt when you disagree or feel the need to challenge a statement?			
4	Examine your thoughts for prejudice or bias that may influence your listening?			
5	Cut the person off or let your mind wander once you believe you've captures the person's message.			
6	Encourage the person to continue, by using responses such as "I see" and "uhuh"?			
7	Attempt to direct the conversation to the conclusion you desire?			
8	Repeat key concepts and essential aspects of the messages?			
9	Feel the need to have the last word?			
10	Maintain frequent eye contact with the speaker?			
11	Assume you know what the speaker is going to say before they say it?			
12	Let your emotions – such as anger and defensiveness influence your reception of the message?			

Are you SHIFTING?

Listening action plan for example:

Being fully in the moment, put yourself in their shoes, repeating back key points to let them know you heard them….

List the ways below:

Emotions are movements (actions/ behaviours) based on our feelings. Which in turn is based on our thinking.
Emotions cannot exist without an underpinning thought that gives it life.

As emotions point directly to a thought pattern, they will affect our ability (positively or negatively) to communicate effectively with our spouse and other significant relationships.

We are not our emotions and they are subject to change so saying *"I can't help it"* is unhelpful to relational growth.
Negative emotions like shame or fear impairs our ability to communicate effectively. Similarly, positive emotions like love supports effective communication.

Creating an awareness of our state and the underlying thought patterns helps us to manage our behaviours and in turn enrich our relationships.

Ask the Holy Spirit to reveal to you the thinking behind your emotions.
Behold, You desire truth in the inward parts, and in the hidden part You will make me to know wisdom. Psalm 51:6 NKJV

Chart showing the 8 basic emotions.

	Basic emotions	How we feel them	Outcome/ Benefit
1	Fear	Apprehension, Overwhelmed, Threatened	Preservation, Wisdom, Protection
2	Love	Affection, Warmth, Tenderness, Compassion	Connection, Life, Spirituality
3	Pain	Hurt, Pity, Sad, Lonely	Healing, Growth, Awareness
4	Joy	Happy, Elated, Hopeful	Abundance, Happiness, Gratitude
5	Shame	Embarrassment, Humble, Exposed	Humility, Containment, Humanity
6	Passion	Enthusiasm, Desire, Zest	Appetite, Energy, Excitement
7	Anger	Resentment, Irritation, Frustration	Assertiveness, Strength, Energy
8	Guilt	Regretful, Contrite, Remorseful	Values, Amends, Containment

There are 3 basic human needs that drive our actions. When Jesus was being tempted in the wilderness, the basis of the temptation that the devil used was to try and encourage him to satisfy these God-created needs outside of the Father's mandated order.

If we don't get our physiological, significance and growth needs satisfied in accordance with biblical truth we are likely to lean on our own understanding. As a result, if we perceive that a need is being threatened by something our spouse or other person has done or doing, we're likely to find ourselves choosing actions to defend or protect ourselves.

Sometimes poor communication is the result of one party feeling threatened in area and has shut down listening in order to protect themselves...

Escape are actions or statements which are designed to get yourself out of a perceived negative situation. For example: Husband complains about his wife not knowing what she really wants, but instead the wife immediately thinks this is a threat to her need for significance as husband might reject her. She therefore goes on the counter attack because it's better to reject than be rejected... She attacks him about the many more things she has against him - stopping his complaint.

Avoidance are actions or statements which, through fear of the consequences, are designed to avoid the impact of those actions. For example: Husband buys a new iPad with money allocated for other things knowing that his wife will be annoyed at him. As this might affect his need for achievement, he also buys her favourite perfume so that when he gets home she's not angry. He gets away with it.

Do you think it's time to stop playing these silly games?
What changes will this prompt in your relationships?

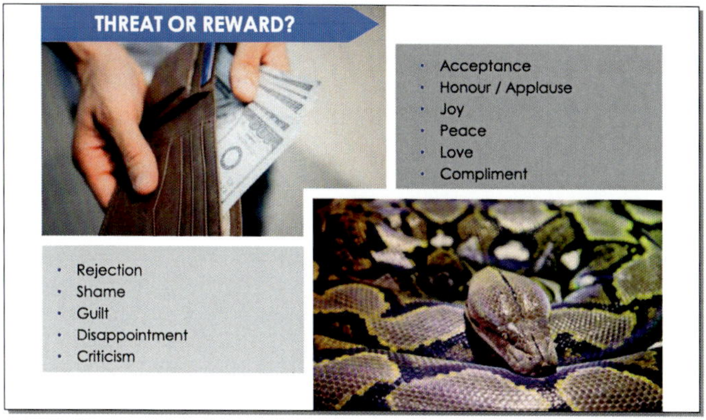

Scientific experiments have shown that when a cell is placed in the presence of a food source and a toxin the cell will always move towards the food, (for growth) and away from the toxin, (for protection).

God created us to move towards things that will promote growth and away from things that will derail us.
This is why he said to Abram *"Do not be afraid, Abram. I am your shield, your exceedingly great reward."* Genesis 15:1b God was maximising the reward and minimising the threat that Abram was feeling.

However, due to our experiences of life, we often get some of these signs mixed up – this is where problems occur in relationships.

It is better to correct someone ·openly [publicly], than to have love and ·not show [hide] it. The ·slap [bruises] of a friend can be trusted to help you, but the kisses of an enemy are ·nothing but lies Proverbs 27:5-6 FXB

The brain exists for our survival. It constantly scans the environment to identify and respond to threats and opportunities, seeking ways to minimise threats and maximise rewards. However, the brain is five times more sensitive to threats than it is to reward so has a clear bias towards protection than growth and is very easily tipped into threat mode. A reaction designed to protect oneself happens almost automatically and instantaneously, before we have a chance to consider it rationally.

Contributing factors

It is important to understand that people from an Afro-Caribbean/ African American backgrounds have had a learnt hypersensitivity to threats (as a result of slavery and racial mistreatment) – which creates higher levels of defensive/ protective behaviours.
For example, your spouse, friend or colleague may be giving you some honest and well delivered feedback only to receive a disproportionate and tense response.

As a result, many long-standing issues just get left for fear of the explosive response. Sometimes the explosive response is a means of escape.

Giving & Receiving Feedback

A feature of a mature and growing relationship is the ability to give and receive feedback. By this we mean constructive and well delivered feedback that focuses on the issues and not an attack on individuals.

Sometimes feedback can be delivered in such a mean-spirited way that the recipient immediately goes on the defensive. This is then counter-productive as the brain is less intelligent in threat state but is open to growth (problem solving) in reward state.

As mentioned above, better are the bruises of a friend as they are ultimately helpful in the long run. It is important to be able to receive feedback with humility and openness to improve – let down your ego-based defensive wall.

POORLY DELIVERED FEEDBACK	WELL DELIVERED FEEDBACK
Creates defensiveness and confrontation	Creates trust and co-operation
Focuses on blame	Focuses on improvements
Undermines the persons confidence and self-esteem	Improves the persons confidence in their ability and potential
Leaves the person guessing	Clarifies 'exactly where I stand' and what to do next
Leaves the person feeling 'judged'	Leaves the person feeling 'helped'

Action Plan

Considering the state of your relationships and your feedback habits:

- ✓ Do you find yourself giving poorly delivered feedback? If so, what actions will you commit to doing to improve this aspect of communication?
- ✓ Do you find yourself being overly defensive when receiving feedback? If so, what will you commit to doing differently to improve this aspect of communication?
- ✓ Be descriptive not interpretive when giving feedback. Attack the issue not the person

When feeling threatened:

- ✓ Try to give yourself thinking space – count to ten...
- ✓ Ask yourself, is my thinking logical? Does it make sense? Am I being biased?
- ✓ Defer giving an answer until you've cooled down. Ask the other person to give you some time.
- ✓ Remind yourself of what has God said about in His word or by revelation?

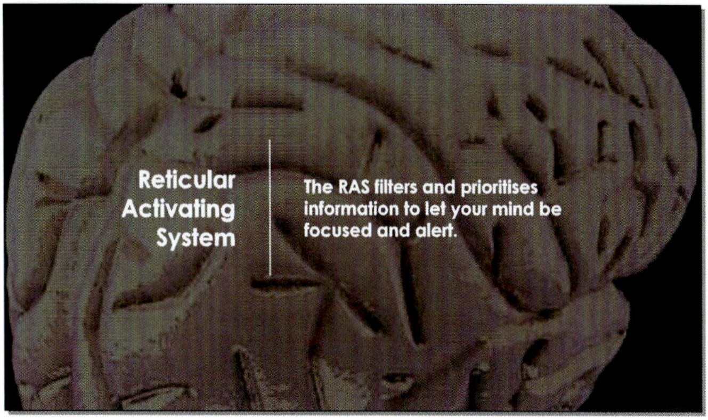

Reticular Activating System - What is it, and what does it have to do with me and moving forward in my relationships?

All the information collected by the senses is received by a part of the brain called the RAS. The RAS is similar to an initial gathering unit that filters information and prepares the rest of the brain for a response.

The RAS is the guardian of our mind - like a nightclub bouncer with instructions to only let certain people in – it is the picker and chooser of information.

It also has a significant part to play in the achievement of our goals including our relationships.
As an example, prior to buying my car, I didn't really recognise many of that model on the road and thought that they were quite rare. However, no sooner than I did my research and decided to buy it, I suddenly became aware of just how many were there all the time. As if it was hidden in plain sight!

Did you know?

The human brain processes 60 billion bytes of information per second.

Your RAS is the automatic mechanism inside your brain that brings relevant information to your attention. Operating like a filter between your conscious and subconscious mind, it takes instructions from your conscious mind and passes them on to your subconscious.
In the case of a relationship, an example of an instruction might be, "look out for danger! I don't trust my spouse" or "watch for him or her – they're always getting on my nerves..." etc.
You will always find what you're looking for!

You can deliberately program the reticular activating system by choosing the exact messages you send from your conscious mind. For example, you can set goals, or say affirmations, or by visualising (opening up your spiritual sight to see what God has said – like Abram with the stars and the sand in reference to his seed).

We can achieve any realistic relationship goal if we keep on thinking of that goal and stop thinking any negative thoughts about it. Of course, if we keep thinking that we can't achieve a goal; our subconscious will help us NOT to achieve it.

ACTION STATIONS!

Instead of focusing on what's wrong with your relationship, focus on the outcome you want to see.

Hidden in plain sight - Colossians 1:16-17 tells us that everything has already been created – visible and invisible - just awaiting our recognition of it. Therefore, programming your RAS by making deliberate decisions or a very specific picture about the things you want to see in your life increases your receptivity for seeing those things manifest by bringing to your attention all the relevant information which otherwise might have remained as 'background noise'.

One of the reasons this is so important is that the RAS will prevent our goals messages getting through to our subconscious if our self-image is not in line with our goals.

And you shall know the truth, and the truth shall make you free John 8:32 NKJV.

This scripture really says that it is our relationship with the truth that makes us free – this freedom is predicated on how much of the truth we know and have intimate knowledge of.

The Lord cannot bring to pass a million-pound vision if all you can see in your mind's eye are pennies.

Your marriage and other relationships cannot be all the God ordained them to be unless you can see it in your mind's eye first.

Unbelief causes your RAS to shut down to the process of uncovering the innumerable possibilities that your relationships can be.

By continually thinking about your relationship goals, working on it daily makes you increasingly attuned to the opportunities around you to make it happen. As you move toward your goal, the goal also seems to move towards you.

Action Plan

I want you to put down the book, close your eyes and as detailed as you can make it, consider the dream, vision or destiny assignment the Lord has given for your marriage and other relationship and say 3 times: "IT'S POSSIBLE."

Hold onto it!

What gets in the way?

What works for us, may not work for them.

It's important to recognise our individual personality differences and preferences. While we can make generalisations as to men are like this and women are like that, the fact is that no two people are exactly the same.

Learn to be a student of your spouse and those you are in close fellowship with. Be interested in knowing more about them, as sometimes what energises and gives us life will deflate them.
Develop an attitude of service – what can I do to support you to be your best?

Frustration on both sides of a relationship can ensue by using the wrong tools to get a result.

In his book, The Five Love Languages Gary Chapman suggests there are five different communication types in how we show love to another.

Finding out what means a lot to your spouse and other significant relationships demonstrates a love that touches them more deeply and meaningfully than anything else.

Acts of Service	Physical Touch	Quality Time	Words of affirmation	Giving of Gifts
Helping with a task	A hug or holding hands	Spending time together in a shared activity	Saying "I love you"	Surprise gifts
Does things to make life easier for them	Sitting close to each other	Taking time to listen to them	Supportive words or compliments	Gifts that show a lot of thought
Helping out even when you're tired	Physical intimacy	Showing an interest in the things they care about	Saying how much they mean to you	Tokens of appreciation

Are you SHIFTING?

What is your spouse/friends preferred love language?

List below (ask if you don't know):

Change requires work.

Energy is the ability to do work. Relationships take work and require the expenditure of energy – lots of it!

Enthusiasm = energy. Its original meaning is possessed by a God which empowers and animates you.

We've become people of the word, but not people of action. We consume the word of God but of do nothing with it.

All too often we give up on a relationship, only for an enthusiast to see the potential and invest... The car pictured is now valued at over £30,000 around 10 times its original value.

By becoming enthusiast of your relationship and the divine purpose contained therein, God will empower you to love even when difficult. In the knowledge that the investment of energy produces something more valuable than its original state.

To restore a broken relationship, you'll have to be prepared to go into the uncomfortable zone and put in effort otherwise you'll just get more of the same...

AREAS TO SHIFT

1. In what ways will your relationships benefit from an overhaul?

2. Ask God to help you see the value in working on your relationship?

Need God's power

enth posses by a God

Being an encourager means putting in a concerted effort into strengthening our mate and those we are connected with to be all God has created them to be.

And Moses said to Joshua, "Choose us some men and go out, fight with Amalek. Tomorrow I will stand on the top of the hill with the rod of God in my hand." So Joshua did as Moses said to him, and fought with Amalek. And Moses, Aaron, and Hur went up to the top of the hill. And so it was, when Moses held up his hand, that Israel prevailed; and when he let down his hand, Amalek prevailed. But Moses' hands became heavy; so they took a stone and put it under him, and he sat on it. And Aaron and Hur supported his hands, one on one side, and the other on the other side; and his hands were steady until the going down of the sun. So Joshua defeated Amalek and his people with the edge of the sword. Then the Lord said to Moses, "Write this for a memorial in the book and recount it in the hearing of Joshua, that I will utterly blot out the remembrance of Amalek from under heaven." Exodus 17:9-14

I've said before that the opposite of love isn't hate – it's selfishness!

A large feature in many relationships is the presence of selfishness.

Our issues. Our needs. Our stuff. We often take an individualistic view of life, when God is more interested in what the team produces… If God was purely individual-focused, he would have let Joshua and Caleb go into the Promised Land ahead of everyone else. Instead he made them wait 40yrs as some things can only be achieved at their fullness when we all go together.

What actions can you take to support your spouse reach the heights God has ordained them?

- Encouraging them not to quit.
- Seeing them as God sees them.
- Giving them a shoulder to cry on.
- Challenging them to succeed.

BREATHING LIFE INTO DEAD THINGS

- Creating the right atmosphere
- Thinking on things that are good
- Speaking things that be not as though they were
- Seeing them as God sees them
- Gratitude

The hand of the Lord came upon me and brought me out in the Spirit of the Lord, and set me down in the midst of the valley; and it was full of bones. Then He caused me to pass by them all around, and behold, there were very many in the open valley; and indeed they were very dry. And He said to me, "Son of man, can these bones live?" So I answered, "O Lord God, You know." Again He said to me, "Prophesy to these bones, and say to them, 'O dry bones, hear the word of the Lord! Ezekiel 37:1-4

Dead things like your relationship can be brought back to life by first creating the right atmosphere and then speaking words of faith in line with God's word.

1. Meditating on things that are good. Philippians 4:7-8
2. Seeing them and your relationship as God sees them.
3. Find something to agree on and build from there…
4. Recognising that working together is a must. It has been said in a popular song that "I need you to survive…" Actually, I don't need you to survive, but to thrive… I can survive all by myself!
5. You are then you become. Everything reproduces after its own kind – the right atmosphere is created by starting to recognise that the relationship already has the seed of success.
6. Gratitude – What aspects of your relationship can you be thankful for?

7. Speaking things that be not as though they were. Speak what you want to see over your relationships instead of focusing on what you see being displayed right now. Based on the Law of Seedtime and Harvest you'll just get more of the same.

A little something to think on:

All the days of the desponding and afflicted are made evil [by anxious thoughts and forebodings], but he who has a glad heart has a continual feast [regardless of circumstances]. Prov 15:15 AMP

Habu 3.17

THE PROCESS OF EXCHANGE

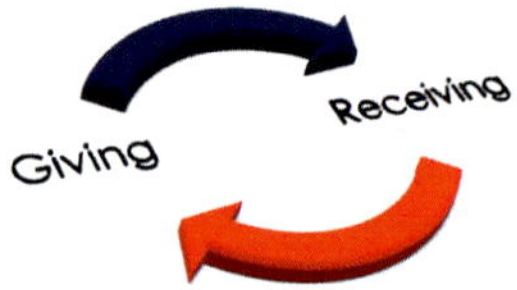

- It's central to growth
- Everything in creation owes its sustenance to the principle giving and receiving
- Not just about money
- To receive something new, you have to let go of what you have

One of the greatest deceptions in the church is the mindset that Giving and Receiving is just about money.

The fact is that everything in creation owes its sustenance to the principle of giving and receiving.

We need air to breathe and because oxygen is ultimately the fuel that allows our cells to produce energy from the food we eat. To receive more oxygen we need to expel carbon dioxide that's built up in our bodies. In the meantime, the plants use the carbon dioxide.

Within our bodies, stress is manifested by shallow breathing – holding onto your breath. Not letting go of poisons. CO_2 is poisonous, leaving it in your system will kill you slowly as you starve your organs of oxygen.

This is like holding onto unforgiveness – it will starve your relationship of the air it needs to breath and flourish.

To experience the best for your marriage and other significant relationships, you'll need to let go of your old mindset and old actions. **You may say they have to change first before I change how I see them; however, you have to let go of the toxic views you're holding onto first.**

Let it go!

What's in your heart that you need to let go of?

A key principle of life is that everything reproduces after its own kind and with that thought you can see how it's difficult (nigh on impossible) for you to get positivity from negativity.

While the earth remains, seedtime and harvest, cold and heat, summer and winter, and day and night shall not cease. Genesis 8:22 NKJV

In giving mankind seed, He gave us the ability and dominion to create a harvest solely based on what we choose to do with the seeds in our hands.

The information we allow into our minds, our thoughts, words and other actions are seeds which when cultivated produce a harvest in your marriage and other relationships.

We all have seeds of love, and the most important soil to receive our sowing activity should be our spouse. However, we often find ourselves at times sowing in another garden. Sometimes issues such as: anger, defensiveness, contempt, stone-walling, criticism, disrespect, belittling, silence and lack of appreciation etc. in our relationships can be the fuel that drives us to invest most of our seeds elsewhere – for example work, church and friends.

Below are some facts about the seeds in your possession.

- You can either sow them or eat them right now...
- Eating your seeds will give you temporary satisfaction if you eat enough but will deprive you of your future harvest.
- Withholding your investments of love and attention will give you seasons of lack.
- Sowing your seeds in gardens other than those you are in connection with will cause a dispersed harvest. Your biggest investment should always be in the garden of those you are in a covenant relationship with.

For any plant to grow it needs 3 components and there's a spiritual parallel for our relationships:

Water - the action of the spiritual arena (we need the Holy Spirit to quicken our hearts and help us to fulfil the word of God). Revelation knowledge.

Air – your environmental conditions. Manage your emotions and atmosphere in your home.

Light – the entrance of **your word** brings light (Psalm 119:130). Speak life over your relationships.

To reap the harvest of great marriages and effective significant relationships takes time and consistent cultivation.

Anything that doesn't exist in your relationships hasn't been desired enough and sowed for...

NOTES

KEEPING SCORE?

love does not keep a record of wrongs 1 Cor 13:5b

It is said that love is blind...

In reality love sees more, and as a result is prepared to see less...

To just think of love as an emotion cheapens it to something whimsical. Whereas, love is the powerful and intentional decision to give of yourself to someone else without pre-qualifying their worthiness to receive or expecting anything back in return.

I've observed a family member that's afraid of needles. The individual would flinch at the very sight of the needle based on the memory of previous experiences. The only problem is that the more they flinched, the more it became difficult for the nurse to draw blood. The nurse assured the individual that it would be OK, but they'd just tighten up. This resulted in their arm looking more like a dart board at the end of what was an arduous process for all concerned!
When someone has hurt or disappointed us in the past we tend to flinch even if it's just mentally, because we are preparing ourselves for the onset of pain. Some people stay in a state of being flinched for years to protect themselves from being hurt.

Another aspect of love is that it keeps no record of wrongs 1 Corinthians 13:5. This can be really difficult because when someone hurts you repeatedly, it's hard not to feel tense around them based on your shared past.

What we end up doing is stacking up pain and resentment that builds into a wall that neither party can see over to interact with the other. This wall of bitterness prevents us from fully experiencing God and each other.

Stacking may cause you to win an argument today but end up losing the relationship in the long run.

Remember, love is about giving without a self-serving agenda in the knowledge that we all stumble in many ways (James 3:2):

- Giving time,
- Giving resources
- Forgiveness

KEEPING COOL...

When He was verbally abused, He didn't return the abuse; when He suffered, He didn't make threats *to cause suffering in return;* instead, He trusted that all would be put right by the One who is just when He judges.
1 Peter 2:23

It's very hard to not retaliate when hurt by a loved one, but this is what God commands us to do.

It's very tempting to fight *fire with fire* or *to give as good as you get*. However, in reality this doesn't promote long-term relational growth.

In challenging us to take a different path in conflict, The Lord is asking us to trust him to put things right on our behalf as He's the judge of the of all creation.

Don't repay evil for evil. Don't retaliate with insults when people insult you. Instead, pay them back with a blessing. That is what God has called you to do, and he will grant you his blessing. 1 Peter 3:9 NLT

Become an expert in reconciliation

The best ways to see eye to eye when things have gone wrong or unkind words or actions have been used – is to become a reconciler.

A soft answer turns away anger – Prov 15:1

Brothers, if anyone is caught in any sin, you who are spiritual [that is, you who are responsive to the guidance of the Spirit] are to restore such a person in a spirit of gentleness [not with a sense of superiority or self-righteousness], keeping a watchful eye on yourself, so that you are not tempted as well. Galatians 6:1 AMP

Let there be no more resentment, no more anger or temper, no more violent self-assertiveness, no more slander and no more malicious remarks, Be kind to each other, be understanding. Be as ready to forgive others as God for Christ's sake has forgiven you. Ephesians 4:31-32 PHILLIPS

INSTEAD OF SEEKING AN EYE FOR AN EYE...
CHOOSE TO SEE EYE TO EYE

Are you SHIFTING?

For example, I thought……. (old beliefs, I now reject), today I'm moving towards (new beliefs)…

List the ways below:

Q&A

What questions do I have?